I0472139

A Bird in My Lens:

Wildlife Photography in Eastern Ontario

Frank Brown

Publisher Information

Copywrite @ 2012 Frank Brown and Maryann Macpherson

All rights reserved. No part of this book may be reproduced or transmitted in
any form or by any means, electronic, mechanical, photocopying recording
or otherwise or any other means, without prior written permission of the
author.
This is a work of fiction. Names, characters, incidents and places are
products of the author's imagination or are used fictitiously and should not
be construed as real. Any resemblance to actual events, locales,
organizations, or persons, living or dead, is entirely coincidental.

All photos were taken near Perth in Eastern Ontario, Canada, using a Nikon D90.

A camera, a lake and a bird. Is there a better recipe for photographic fun? If there was ever a good excuse, sorry, I mean a reason, for leaving chores unfinished, surely it's the chance to catch a glimpse of a baby loon trailing in his mother's wake, and to record that moment to re-visit it over and over, to be able to share it with others. Or to look overhead, click and preserve the image of a wood duck backwinging in for a landing.

There's nothing simple about bird portraits. You need patience to allow the scene to unfold, patience to wait for the instant when conditions are ideal, the image sharp, the light just so, the background complimentary.

Frank Brown's photos of the birds near his home remind us that it isn't necessary to travel to remote pockets of wilderness to enjoy the beauty of our world. His images, the results of years of experience and an artistic vision, allow us the freedom to truly see these birds in all their fascinating complexity, to appreciate the curve of a beak, the softness of a feather, an intensely focused expression, the water droplets glistening on a beak. We try to retain an impression of these birds when we're fortunate enough to see them, but our memories can only give us fleeting glimpses, a remembrance of enjoying watching a loon glide by, or keeping company with a partridge down by the woodpile. We need photographs to truly be aware of what we've seen, to make a perfect moment last longer than a mere moment.

Frank once wrote that "I never know what I'm going to take a photo of next, and that is part of the fun." It's certainly been fun for me; I've had the great pleasure of enjoying Frank's photos for years. I am pleased and excited to share his photographs with you.

Maryann Macpherson

A Bird in My Lens

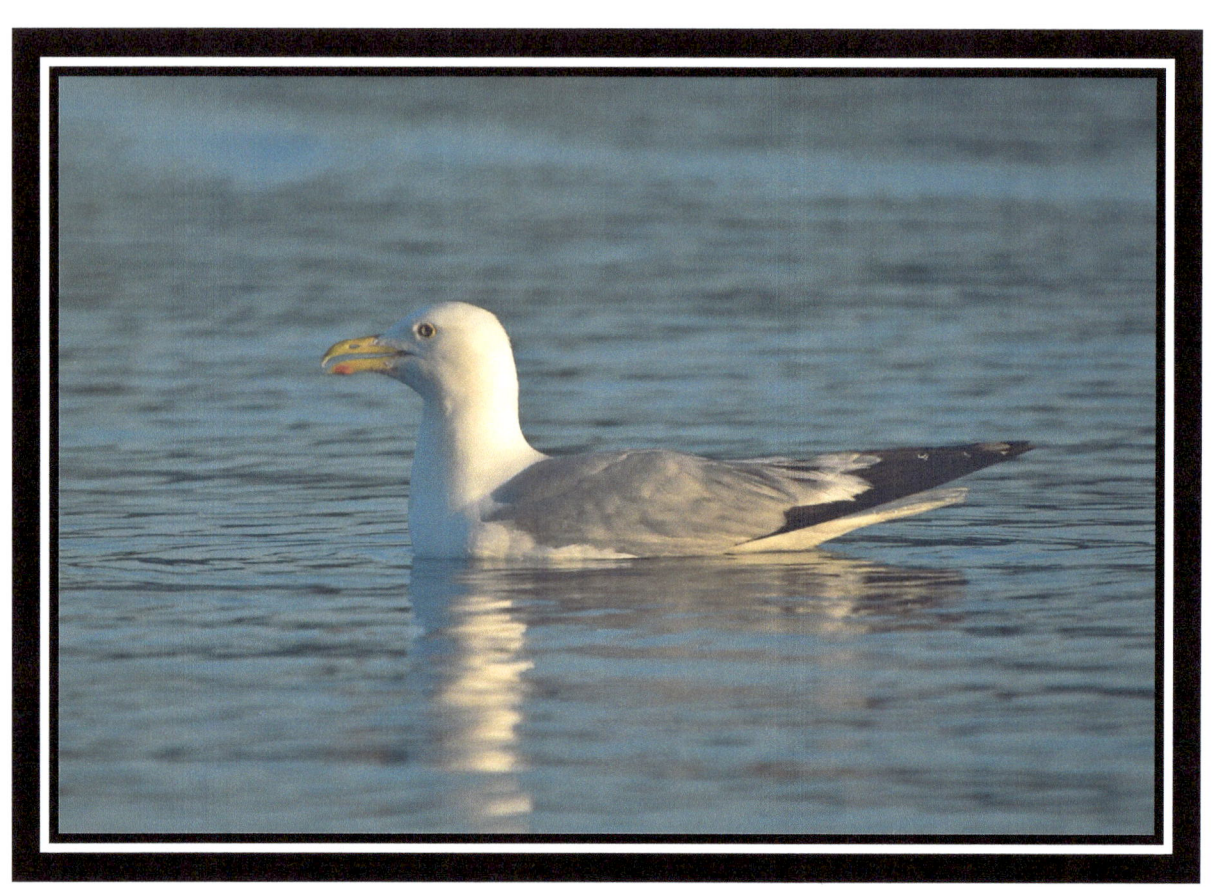

Seagull

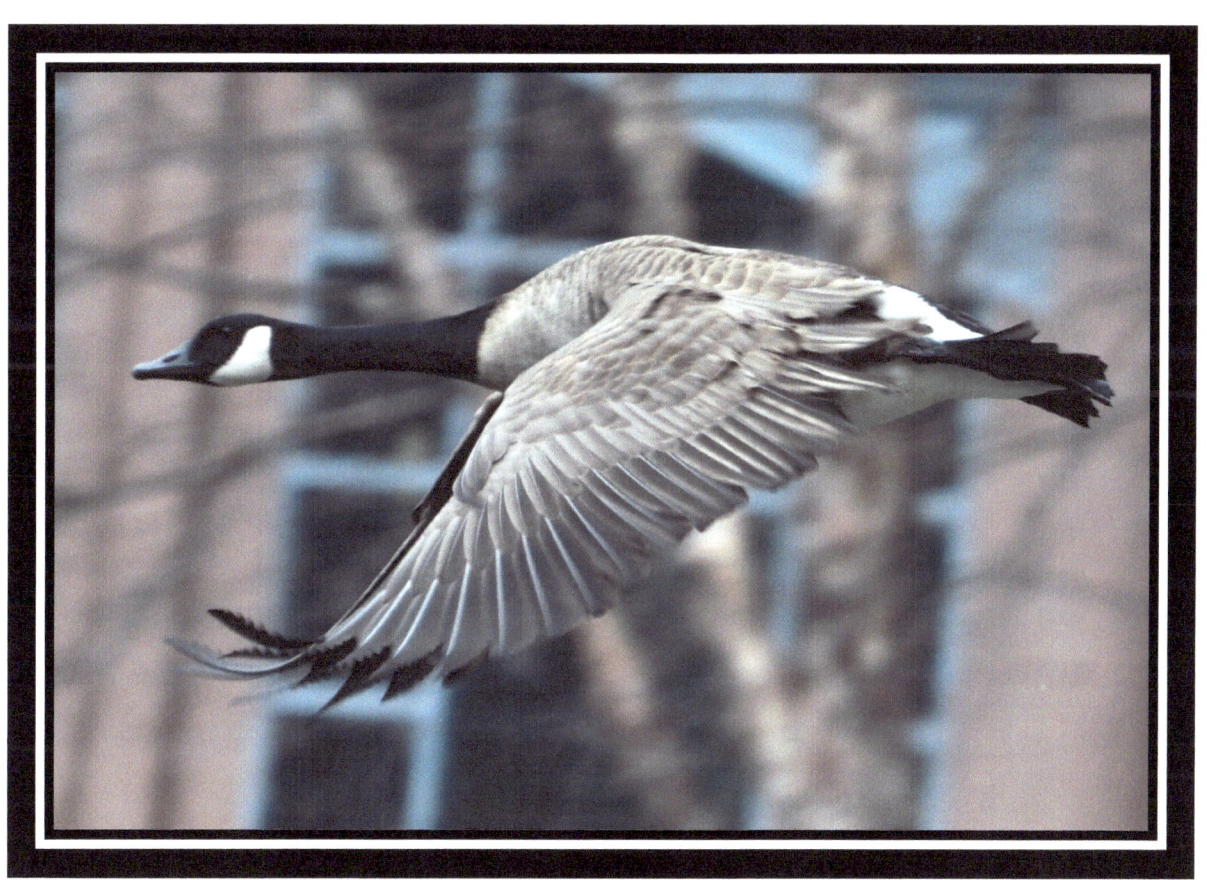

Canada Goose

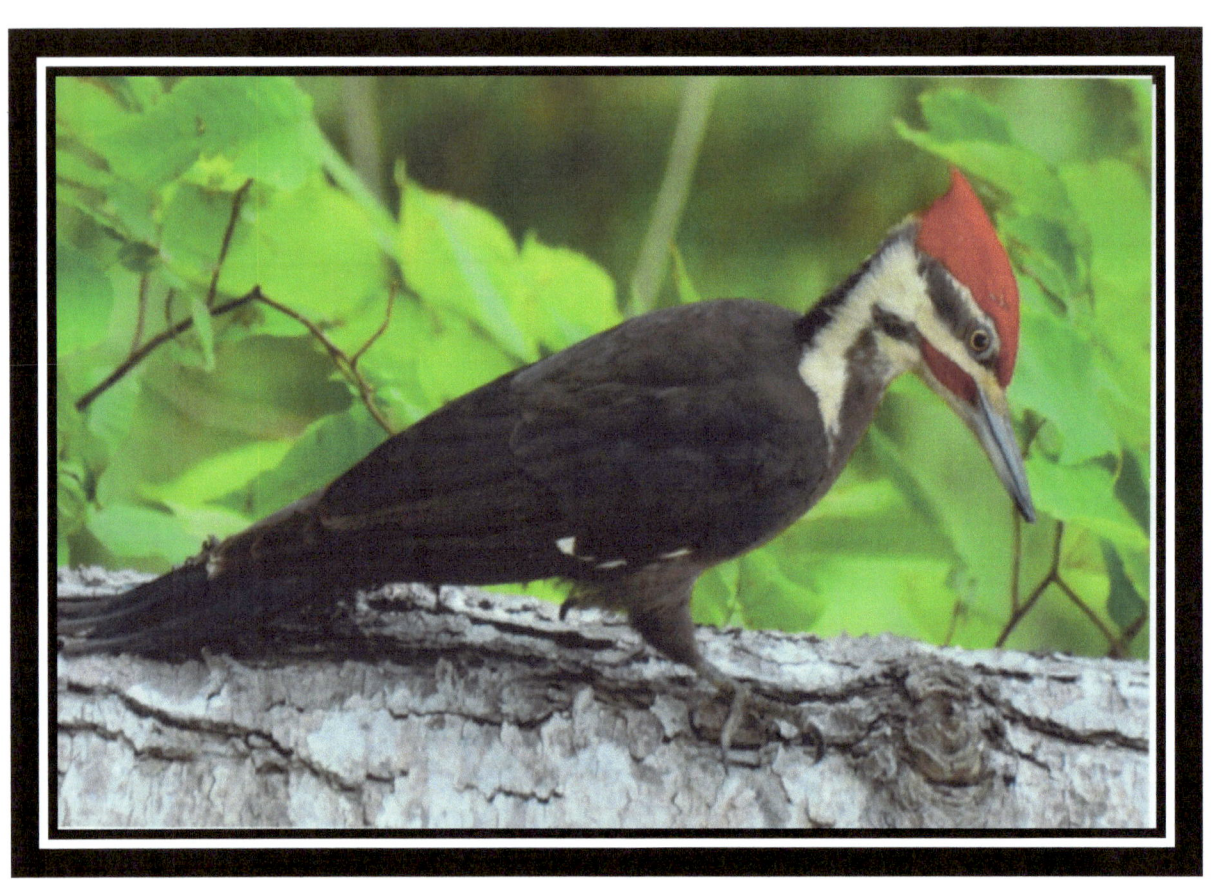

Pileated Woodpecker

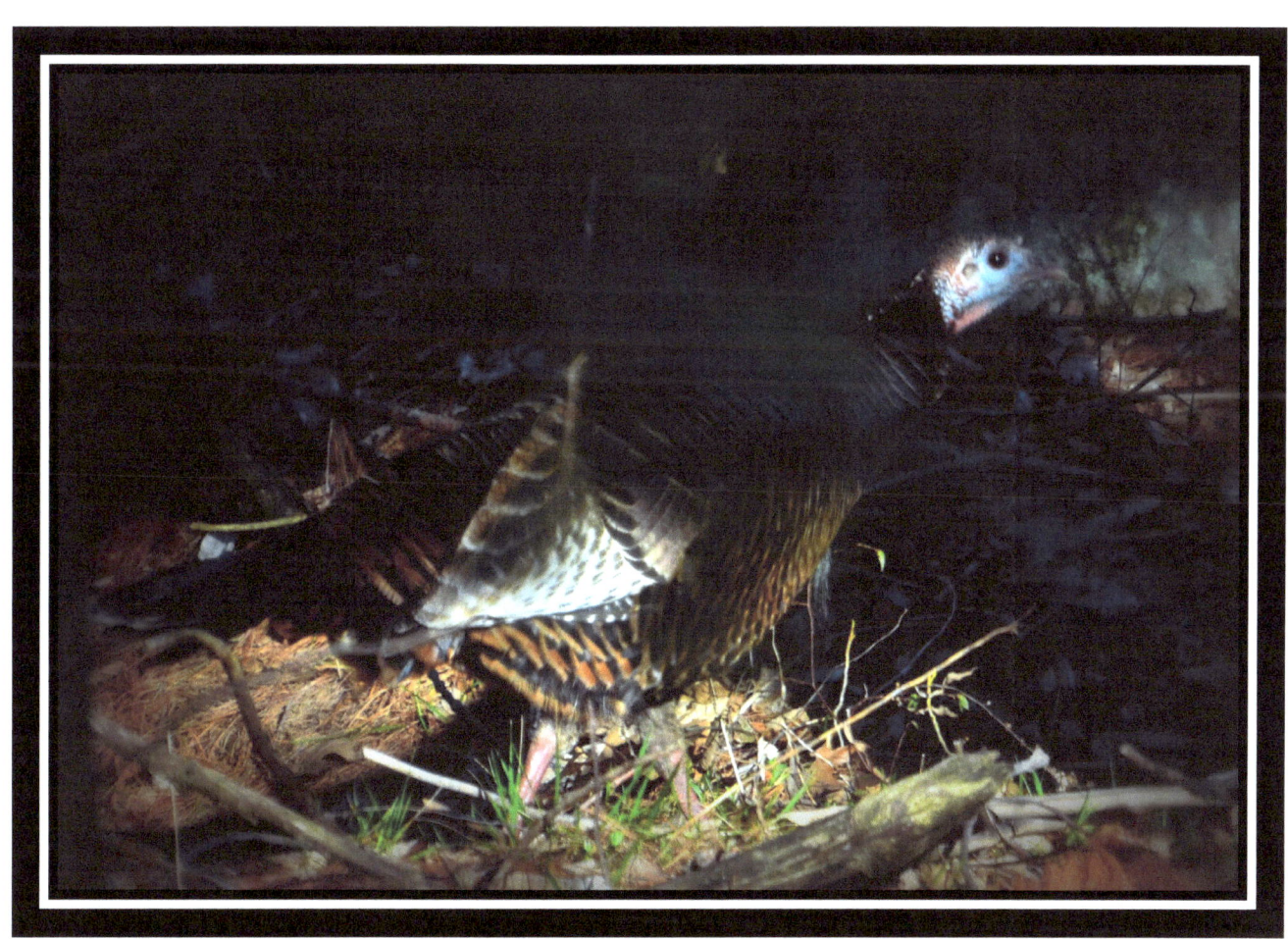

Turkey

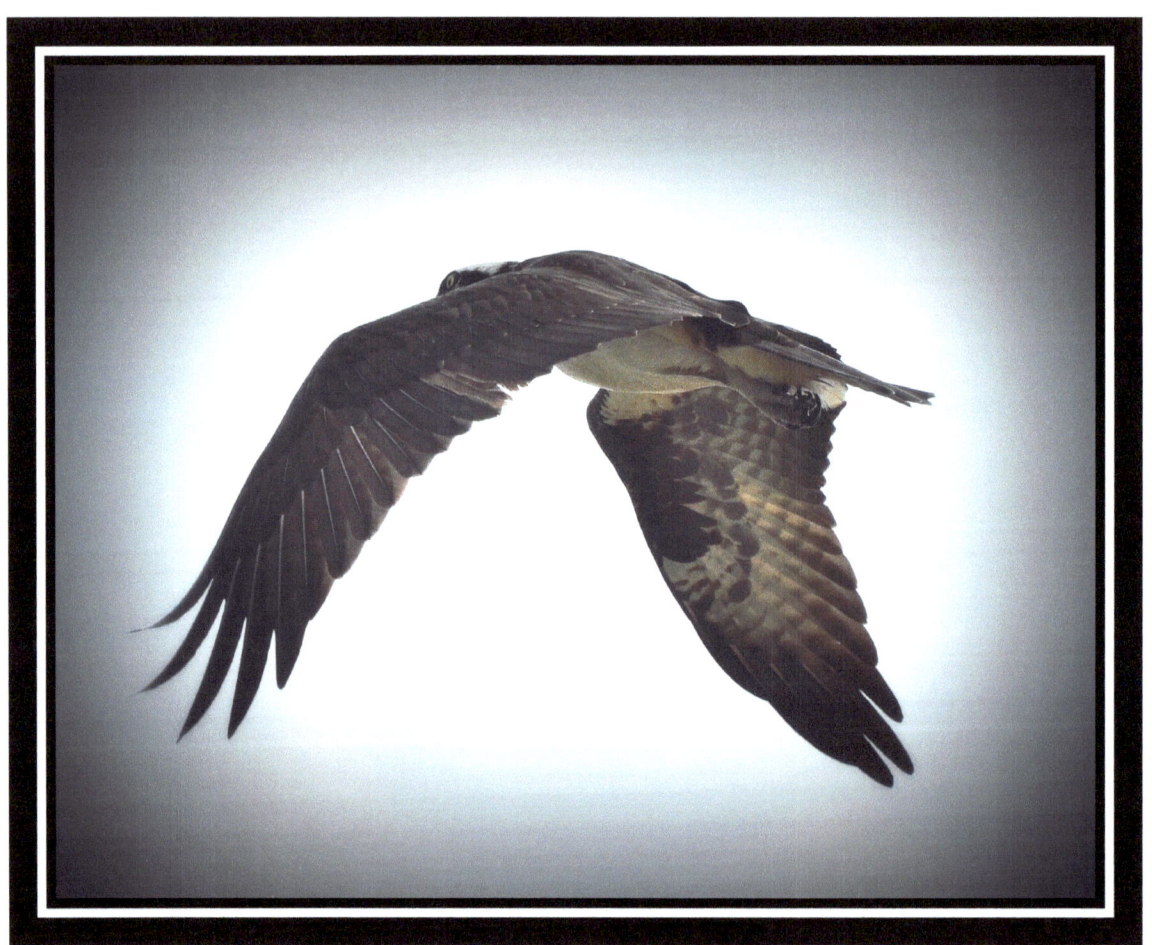

Osprey

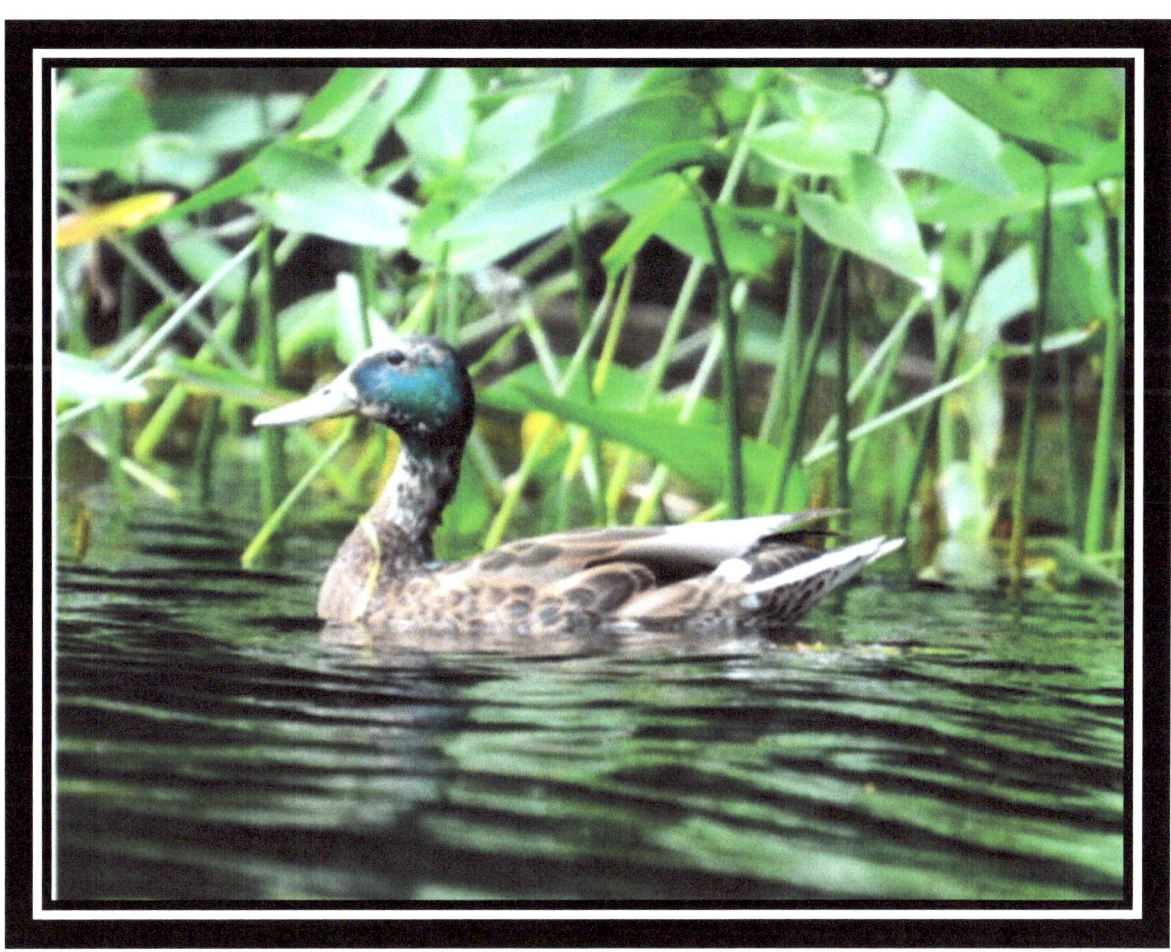

Mallard

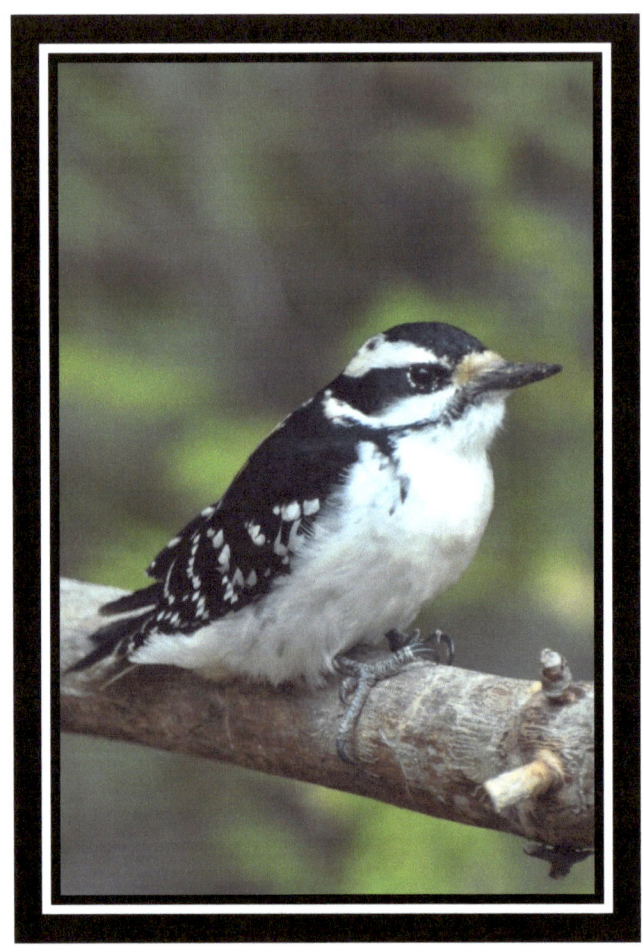

Downey Woodpecker

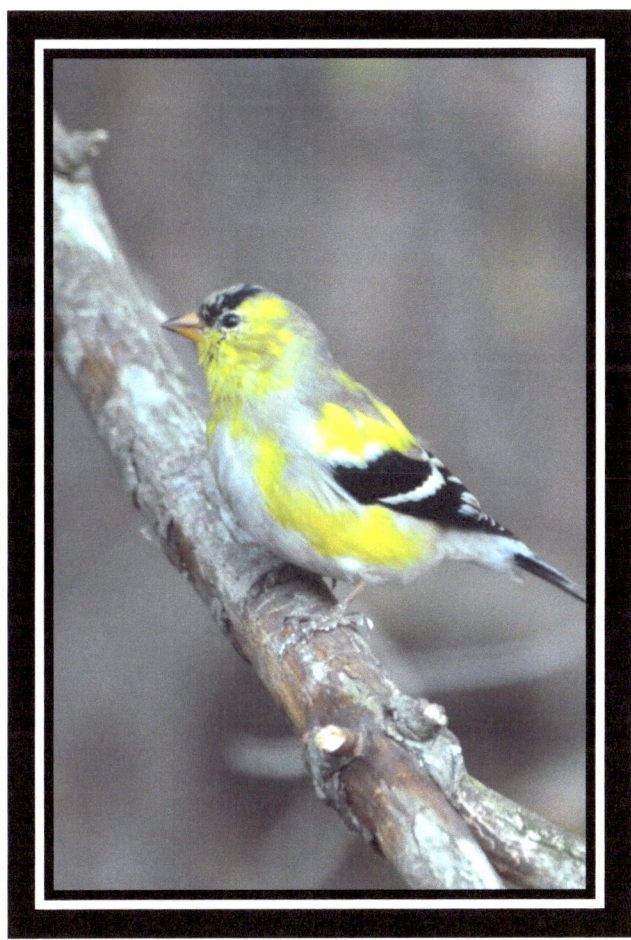

Goldfinch

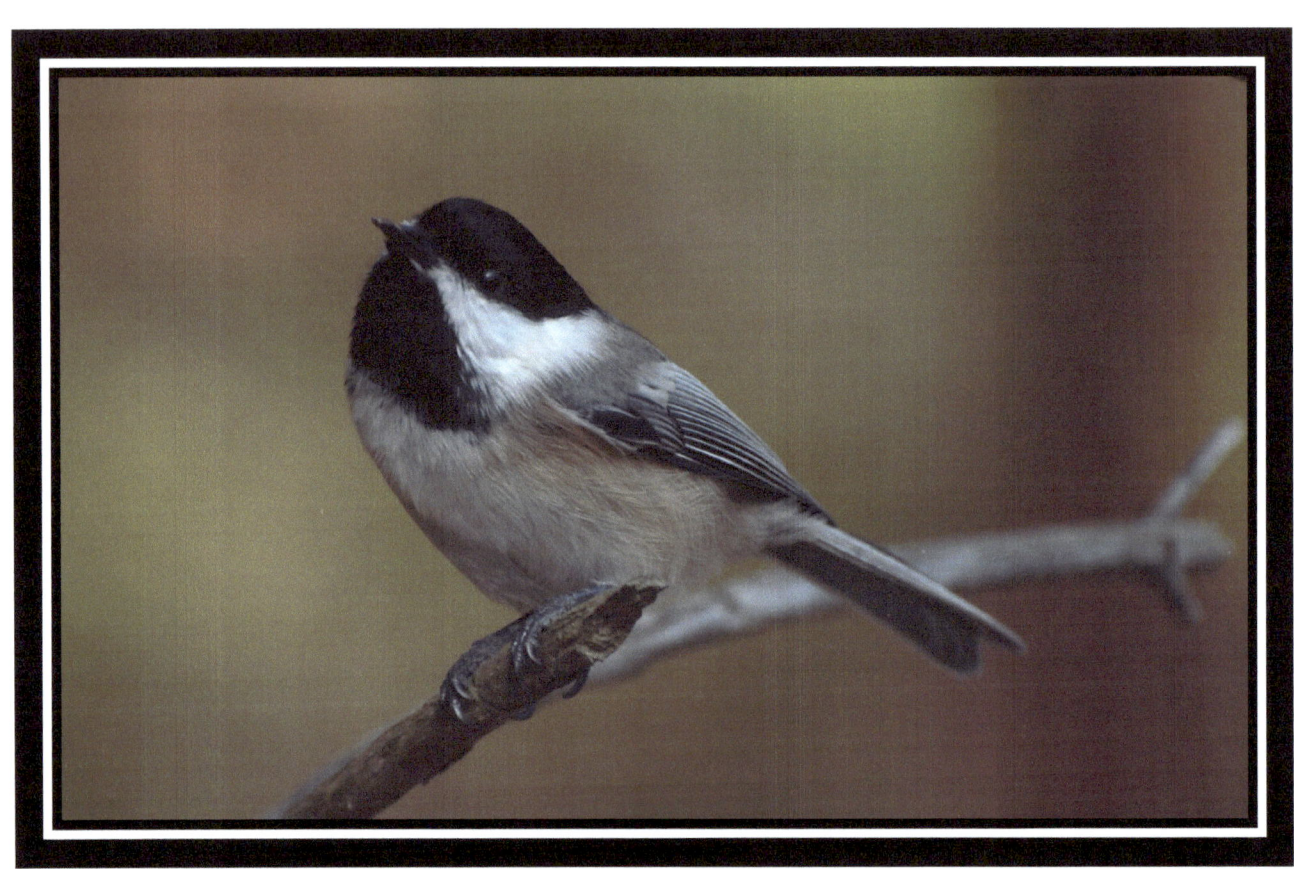

Chickadee

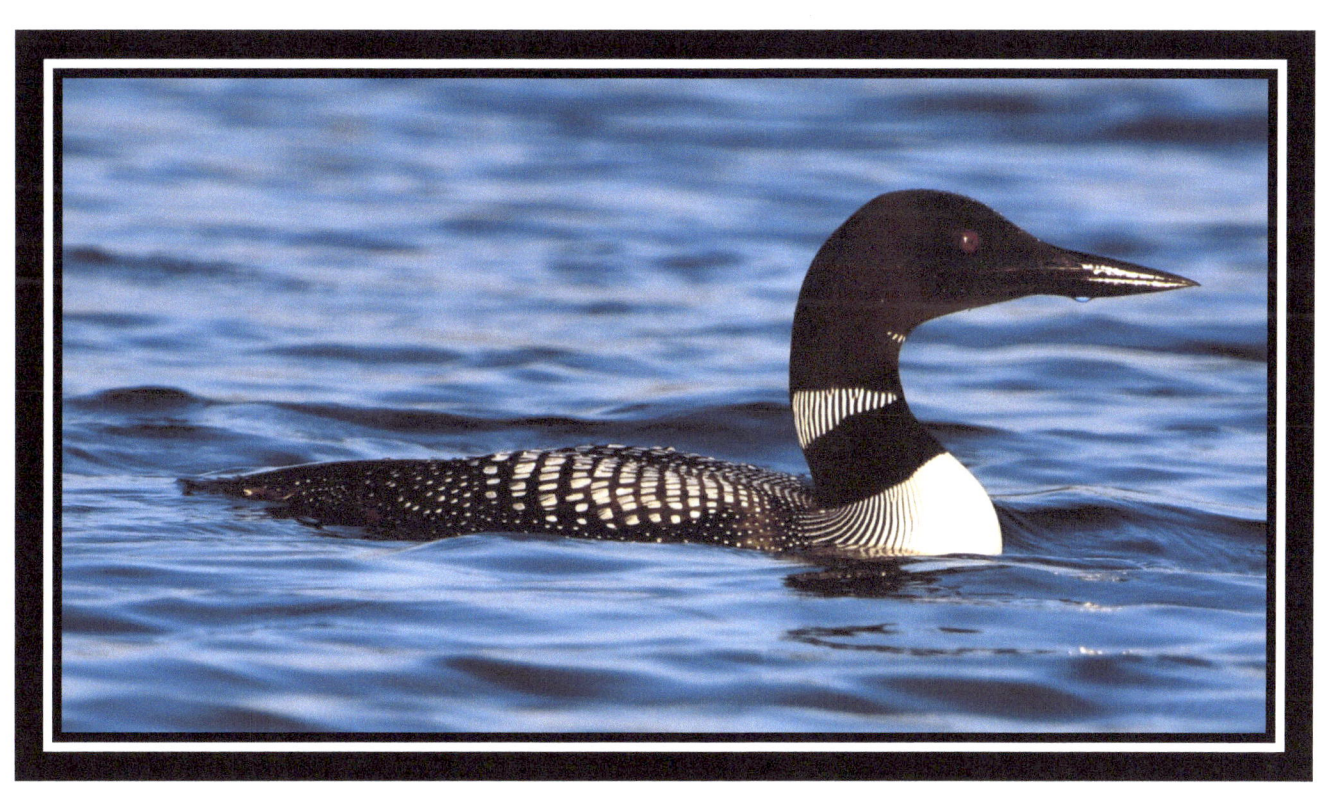

Loon

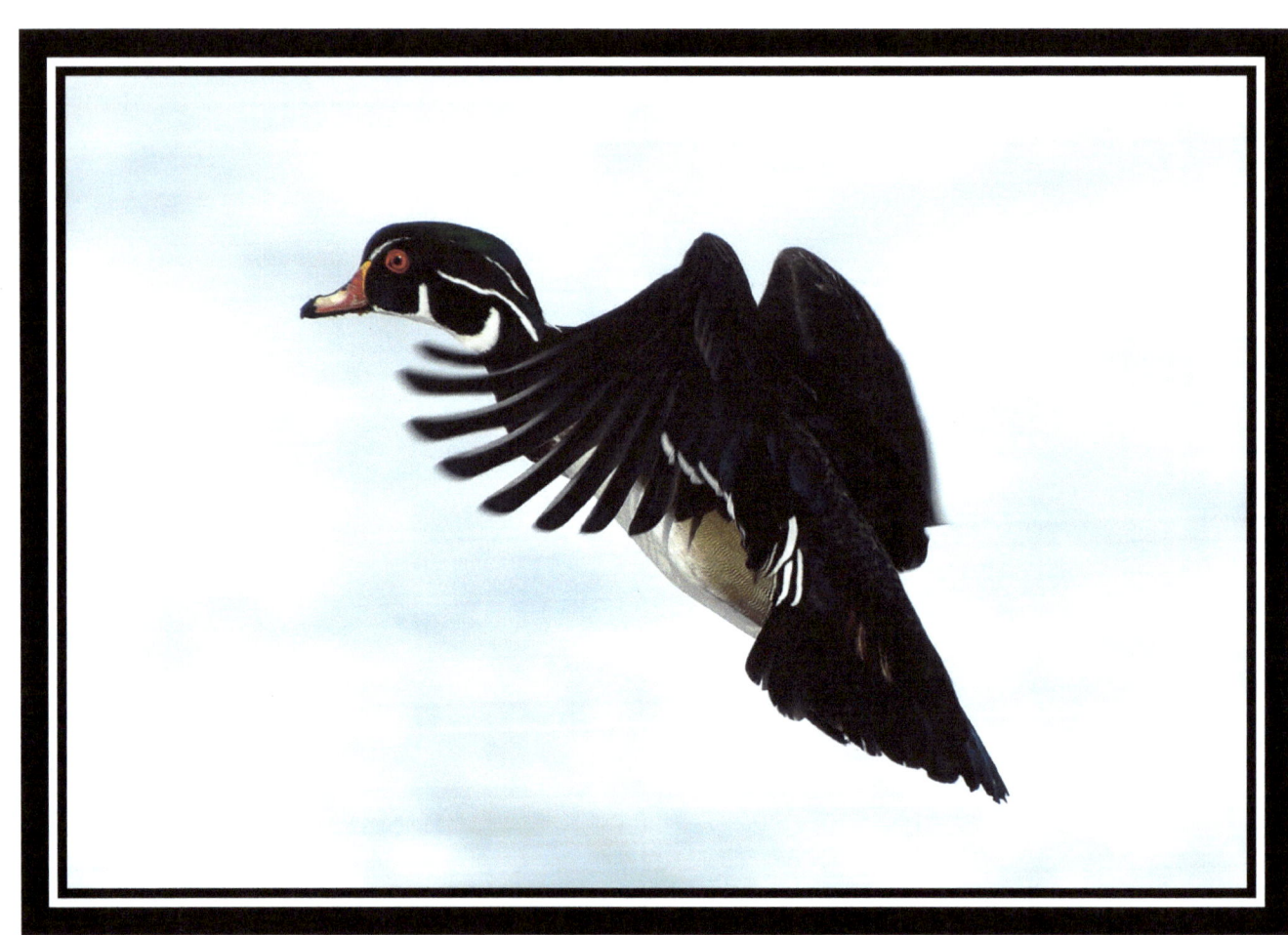

Wood Duck

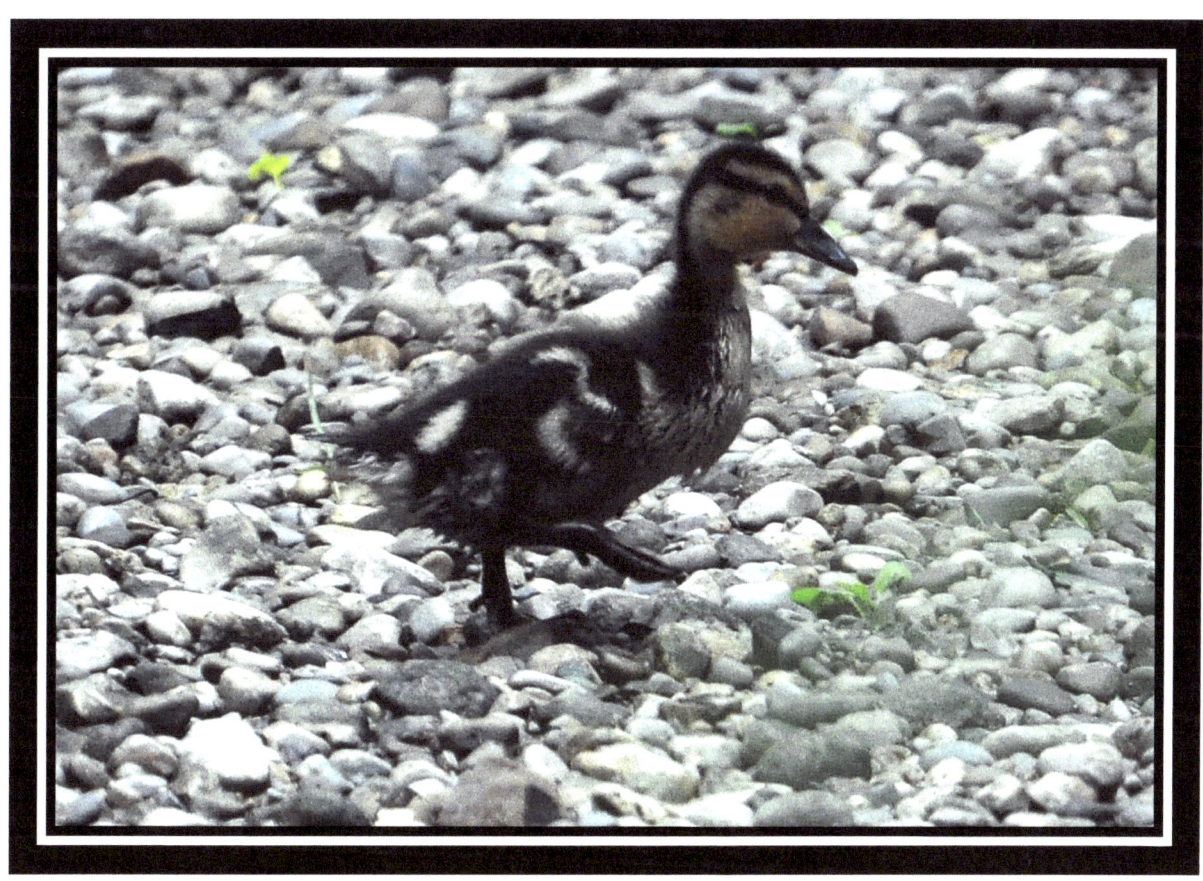

Duckling

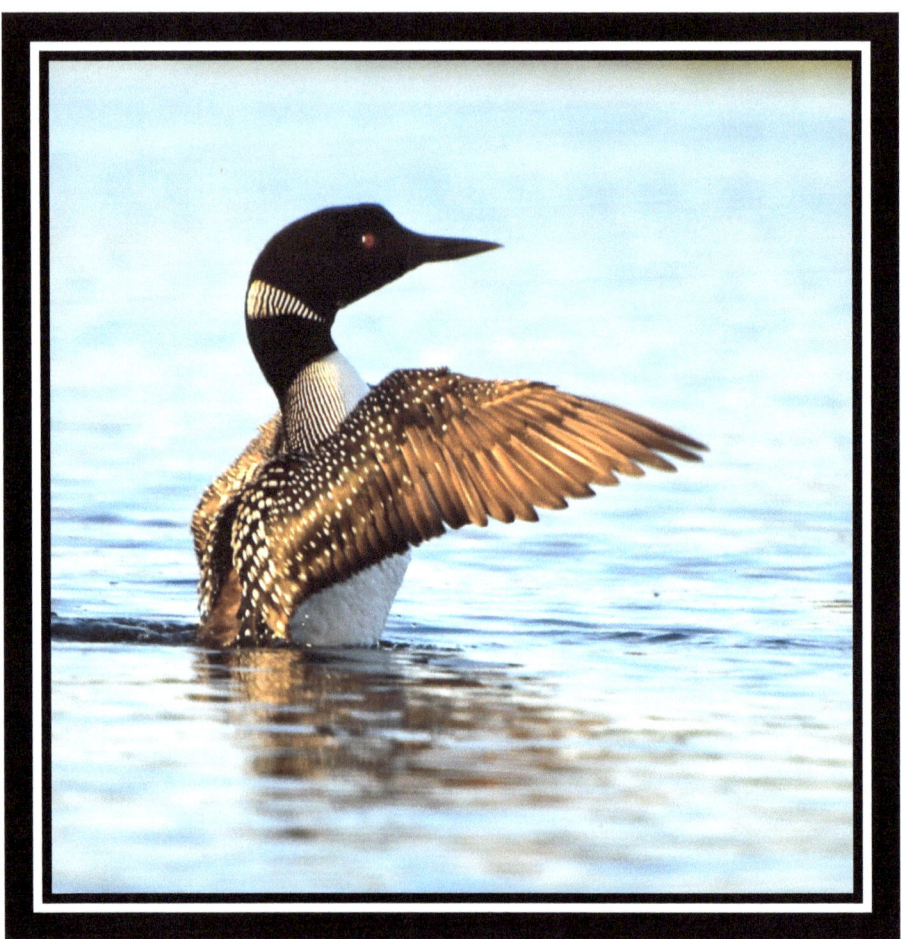

Loon

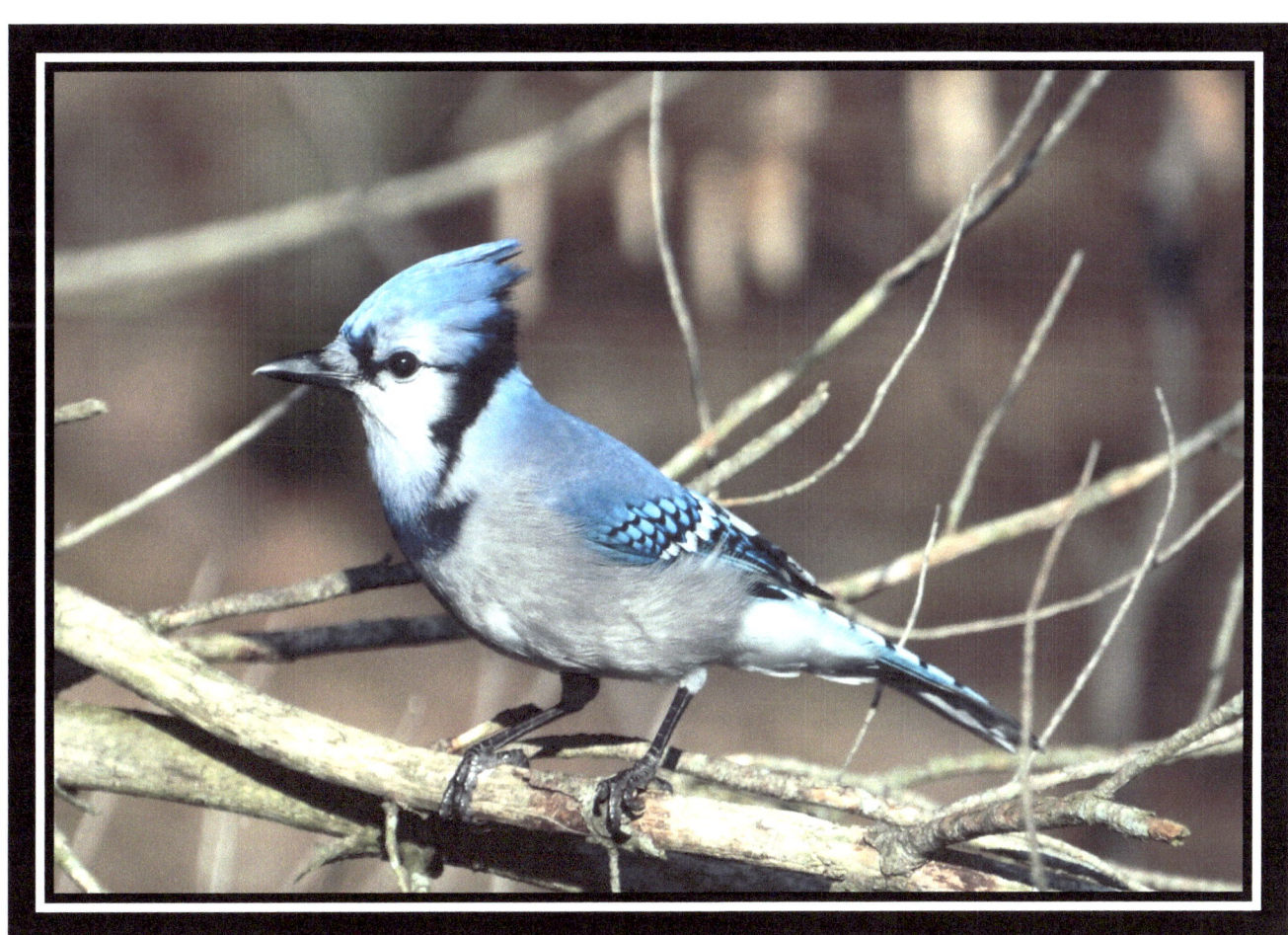

Bluejay

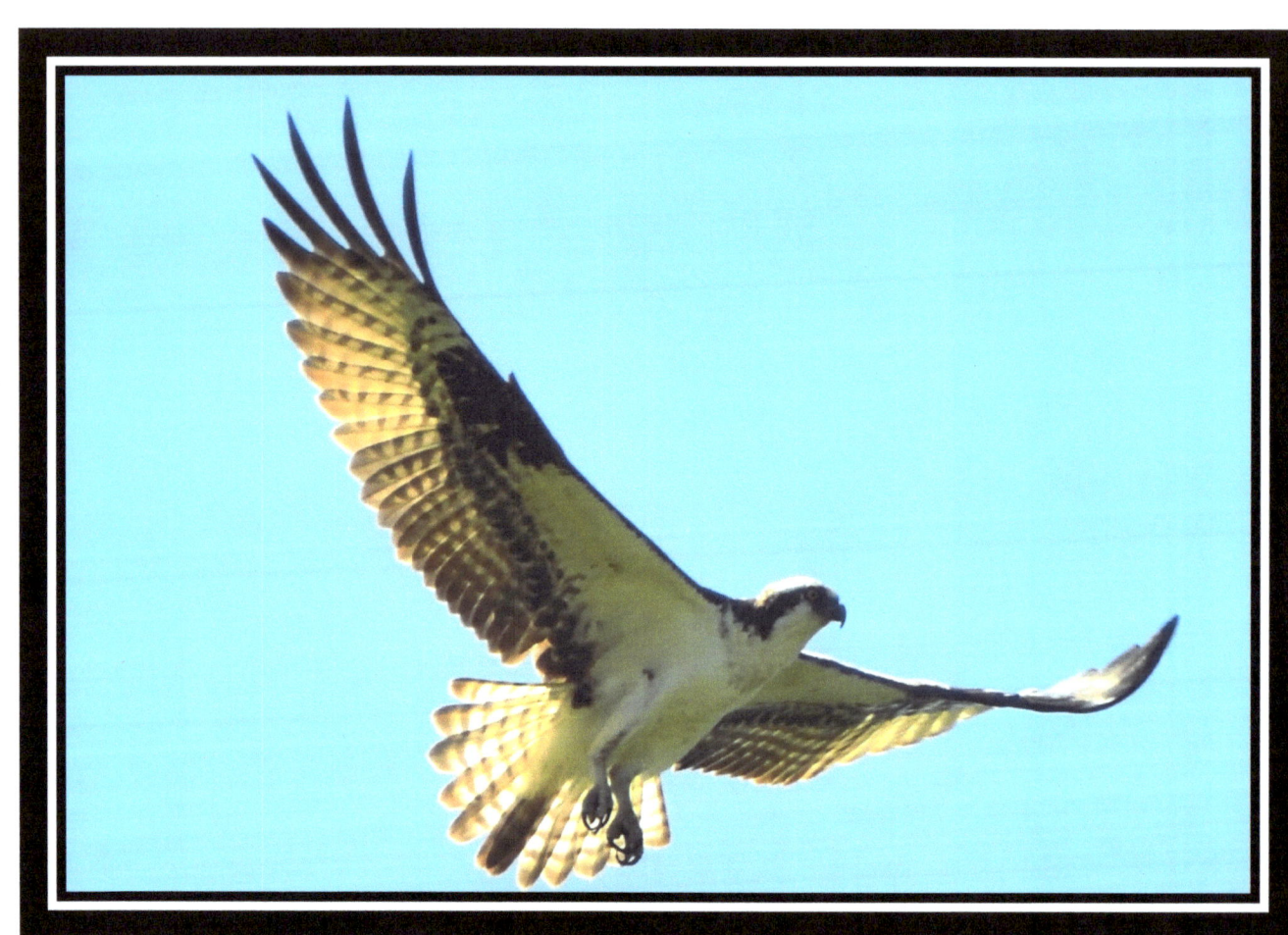

Osprey

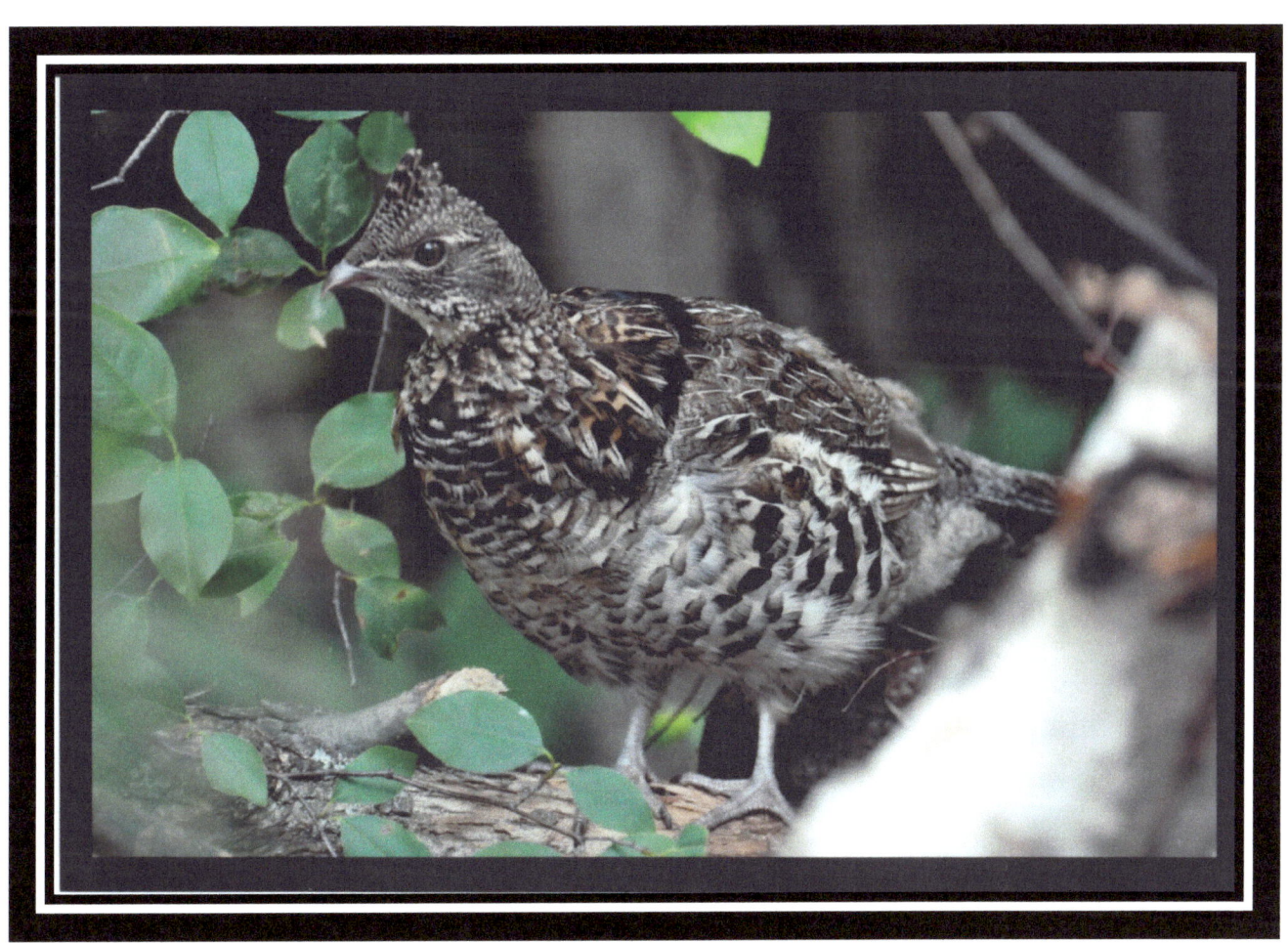

Partridge

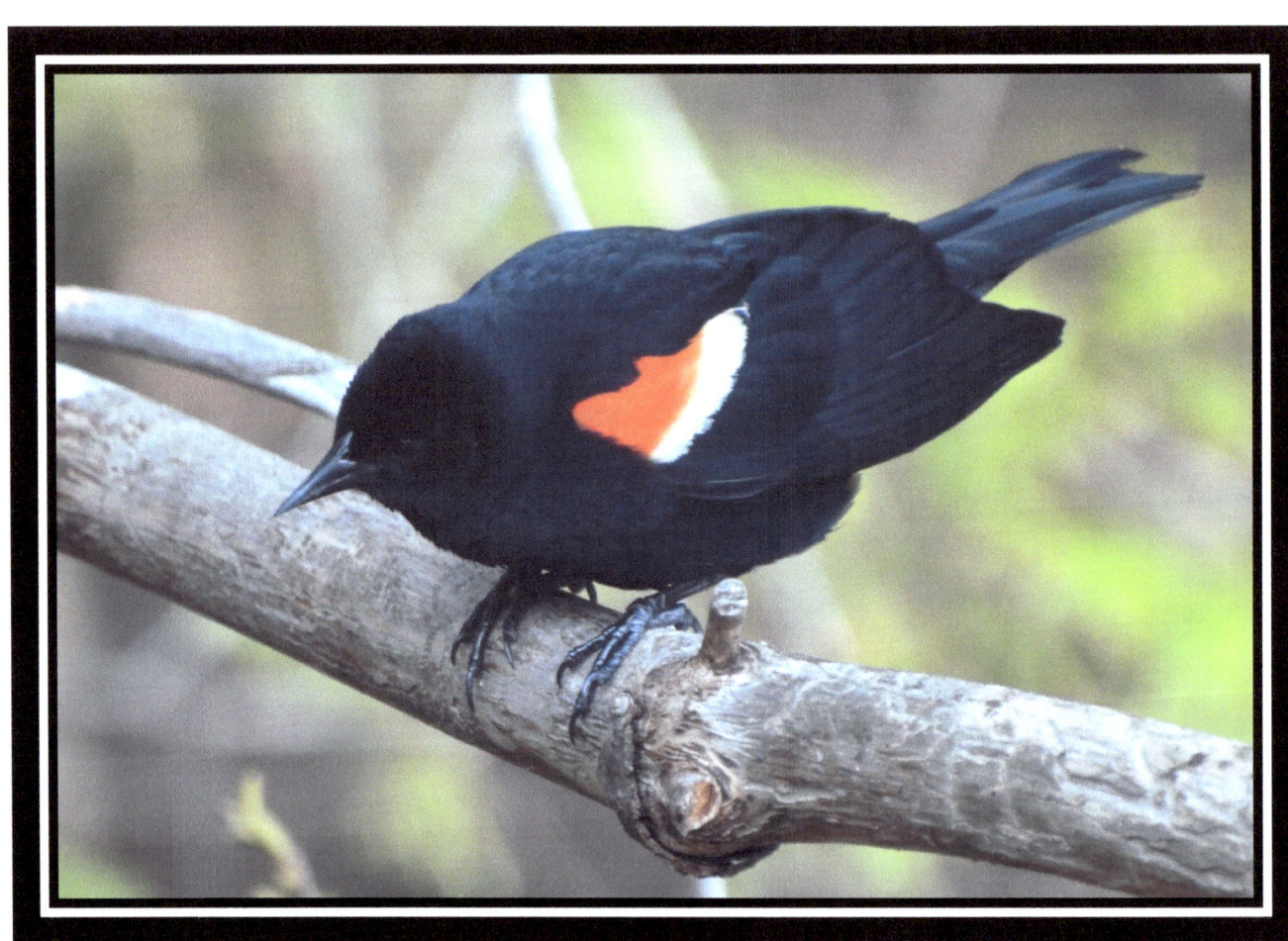

Redwing Blackbird

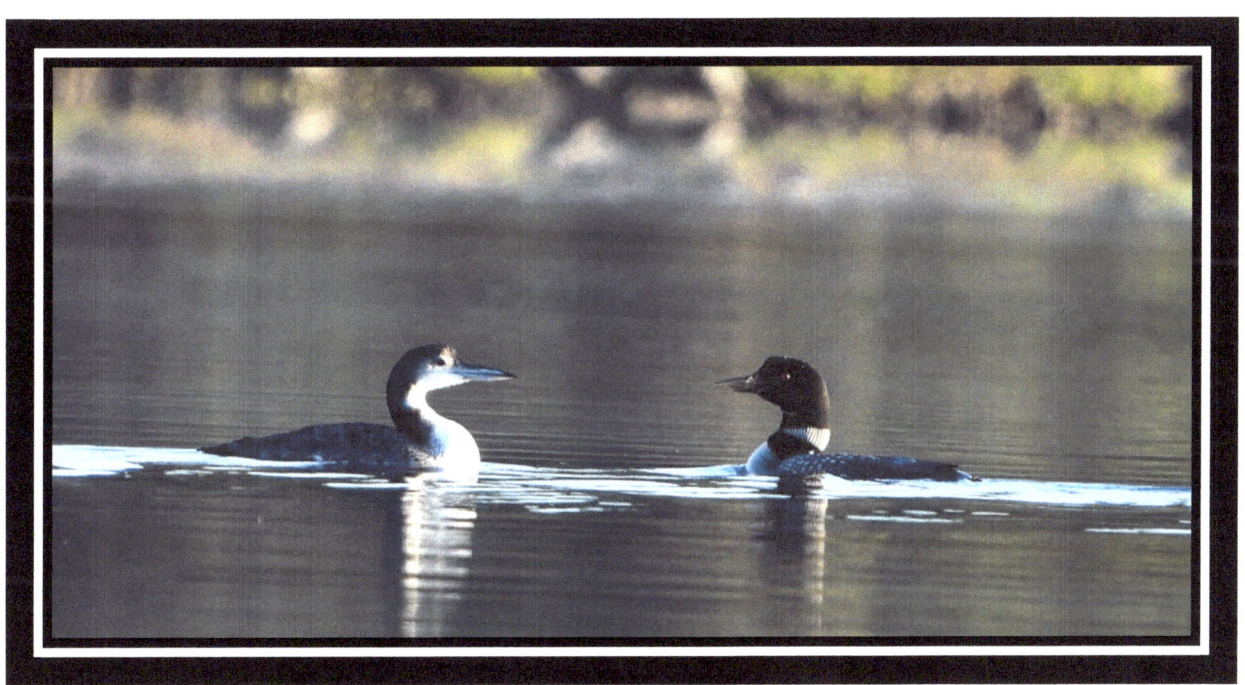

Red Throat Loon, Common Loon

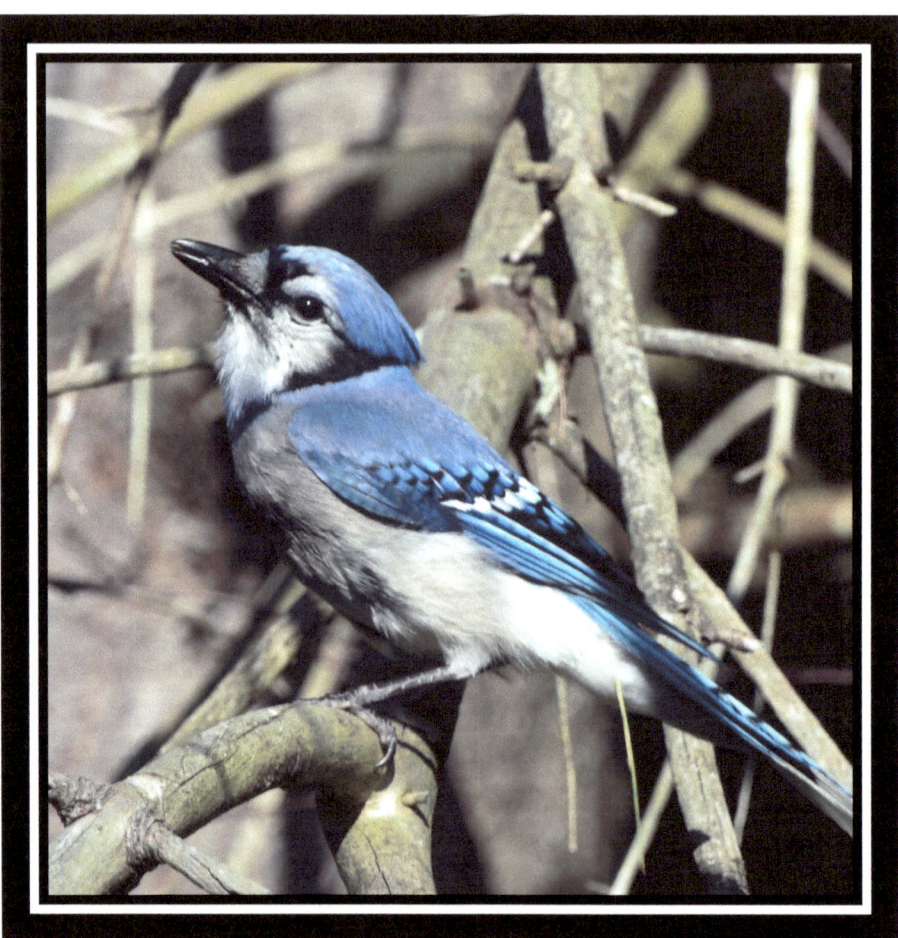

Bluejay

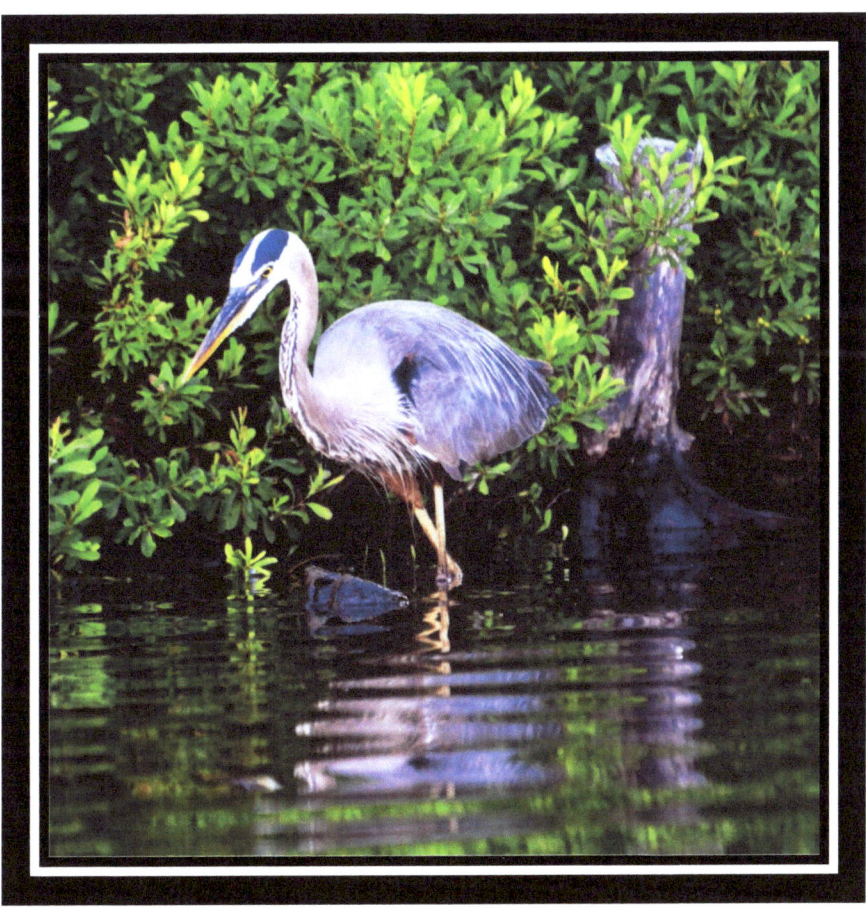

Heron

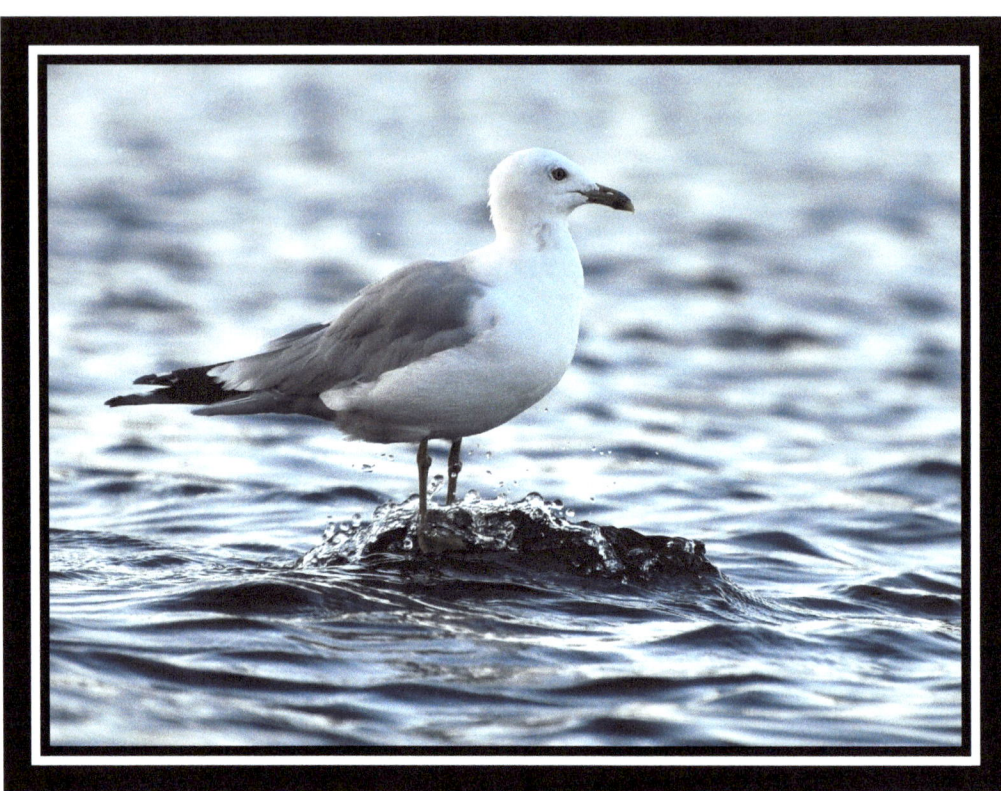

Seagull

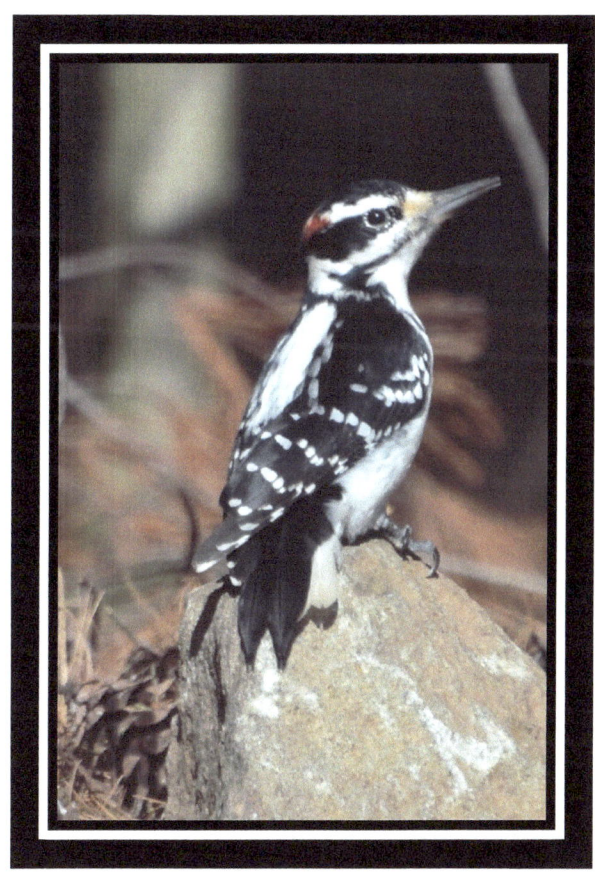

Woodpecker

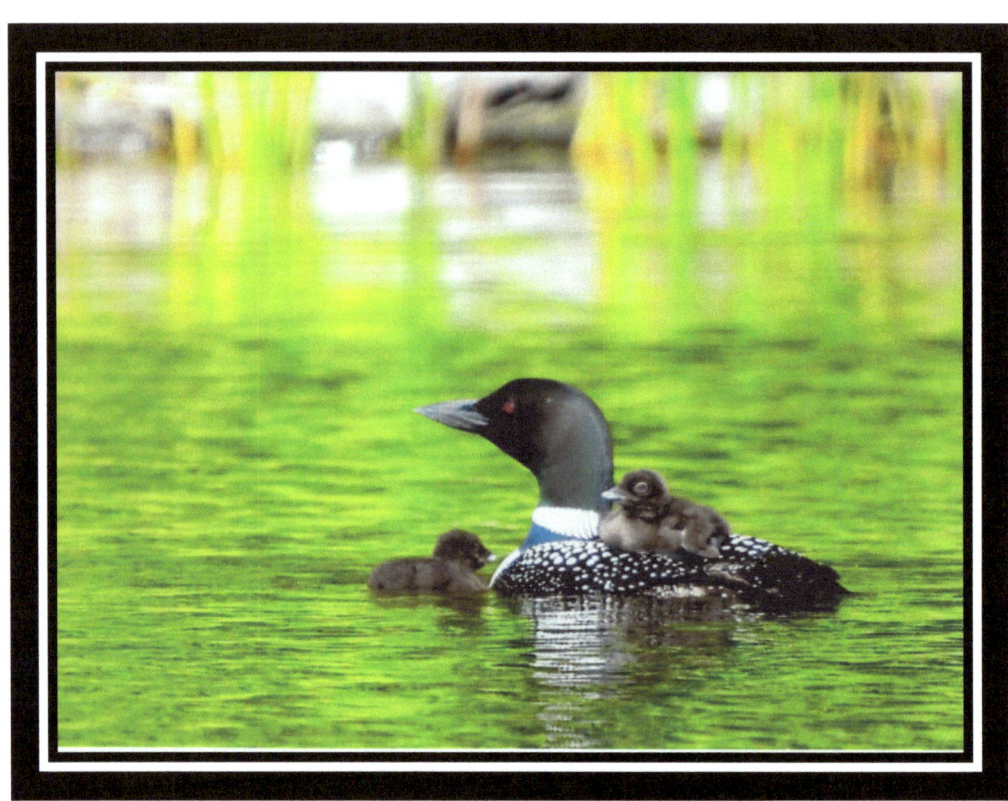

Loon and chicks

A final thought–

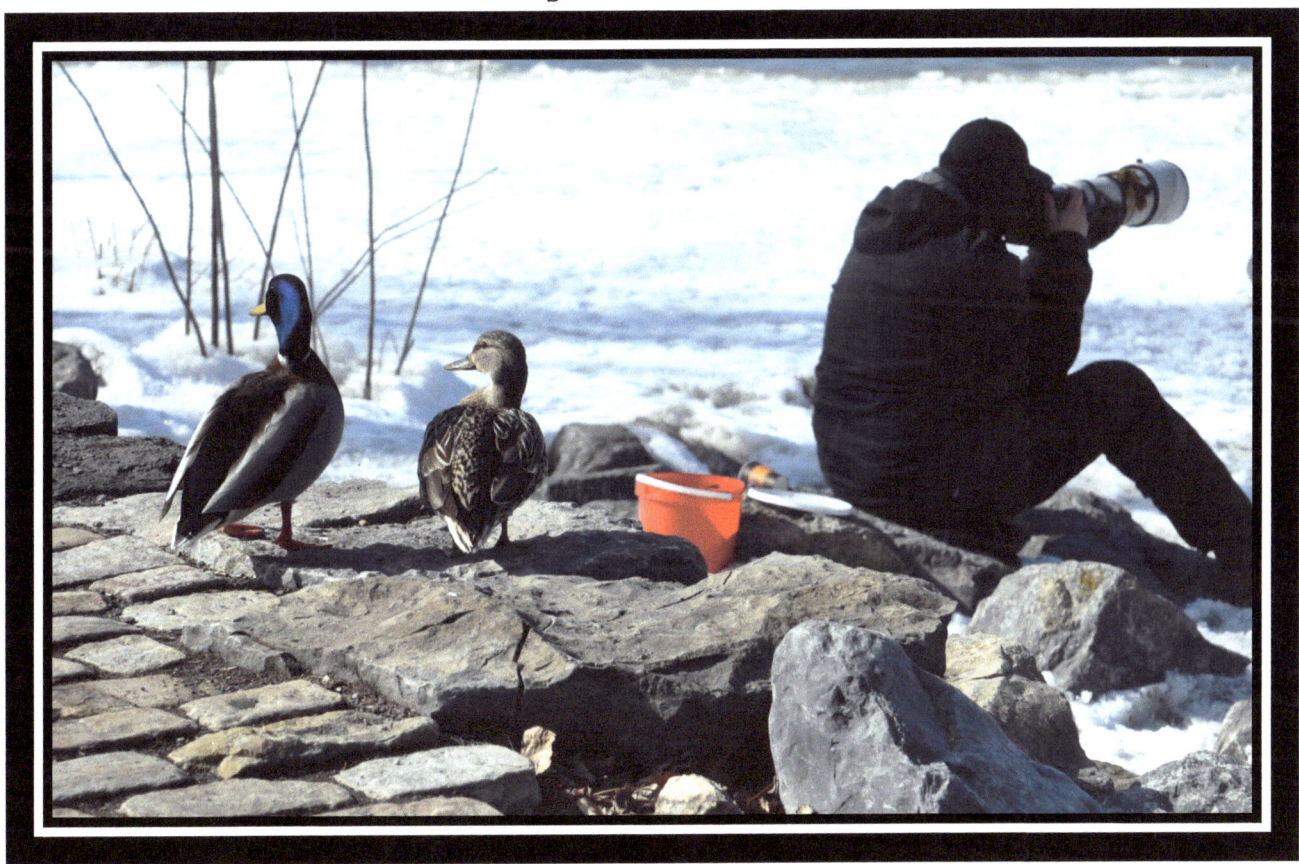

sometimes you can be a little too focused on what's in front of you.

www.ingramcontent.com/pod-product-compliance
Lightning Source LLC
Chambersburg PA
CBHW041306180526
45172CB00003B/993